THE PIER

Volume II

CW01431707

The Pierian is a journal of poetry
published annually

EDITORS: **Max Roland Ekstrom**
Keeley Schell

Order issues and read the latest poetry released every month at
www.thepierian.org. Poetry submissions welcome at our website. Contact
info@thepierian.org for all other inquiries.

ISSN 2835-5806

THE PIERIAN

is pleased to announce its poetry prize winner, published in this volume.

2024 ALEXANDER POPE AWARD OF $105

The Pierian editors distinguish one poem each year published via regular, blind submission which best embodies its ideals, named in honor of Alexander Pope (1688–1744), poet, editor, and popularizer of Greek classics.

DAVID ELLIOT EISENSTAT
for
"THE GHOST OF LI BAI ON MONT VENTOUX"

TABLE OF CONTENTS

FOREWORD

Exegi monumentum aere perennius: I have built a monument more lasting than bronze. Horace's famous meditation on his poetry proved true, but for most poets and poetic publications, the aspiration to long-lasting fame and relevance is only a dream. We are extremely grateful to have persisted through two years of publishing poetry online (a notoriously less-lasting-than-bronze medium, as the recent attacks on the Internet Archive highlight) in order to bring you this second physical artifact, *The Pierian* volume 2.

As *The Pierian* does not solicit submissions, each poem we read is a delightful surprise. Reading submissions is one of my favorite parts of being an editor, matched only by the engaging puzzle of arranging the poems into the print issue. This year, we read a great volume of great poetry.

Some poetry is great but "not for us;" we wish those poets the best at other journals. On the other hand, when a poem stands out for its allusion to a poetic tradition, its celebration of landscape, or its experimentation with form, we know we have a Pierian publication at hand. Each web issue saw a different assortment of these and related themes. Drawing them together into the annual omnibus edition, I can see that we published a great deal of poetry inspired by science and nature this year. There were some intriguing explorations of meter, form, ekphrasis and allusion. The conversations about translation that imbued our monthly newsletters for Pierian Patreon supporters were inspired by poems that engaged with the poetry, arts and language of far-flung cultures.

Considering these thematic strands, the standout poem in this year's issue, winner of the 2024 Alexander Pope Award, is David Elliot Eisenstat's "The Ghost of Li Bai on Mont Ventoux." This poem melds allusions to monumental figures of both the Eastern and Western traditions within the context of a classic sonnet. The poem portrays Petrarch failing to observe the nature around him because of his preoccupation with text.

One of the delights of being an editor is to publish a poem that enlightens a perspective differing from one's own. Reading Petrarch's "Ascent of Mont

Ventoux" and his Latin philosophical writings under the tutelage of Professor Ron Witt at Duke at the turn of this century made me no less interested in the landscape than in Augustine's *Confessions*; perhaps an affection for Provençal wines is the most lasting relic of that study. Petrarch was an intensely complex figure, straddling a past and a future he was instrumental in bringing about. Our award-winning poem addresses him from the perspective of a long-dead Tang dynasty poet who is no less complex, to great effect.

The project of running a literary magazine continues to be a valiant struggle. Each month, Max and I dedicate many hours to selecting the best new verse, reflecting on it for the newsletter, and engaging with the literary community. We hosted virtual events on workshopping poetry and on the impact of Sappho on the lyric tradition.

We are deeply indebted to all of you who help bring about the success of this endeavor: our readers, Patreon supporters, prospective poets, and above all our contributing authors. We hope you know how much your connection to our young project means to us. Please keep in touch.

David Elliot Eisenstat

THE GHOST OF LI BAI ON MONT VENTOUX

[Li Bai] is said to have been drowned by leaning over the gunwale of a boat in a drunken effort to embrace the reflection of the moon.
    —Herbert Allen Giles, *Gems of Chinese Literature: Verse*

Petrarch, you've dreamed of seeing to the edge
of Spain: must you hate each step up the ridge?
Cursing the briars, you pass the poppies by.
Cursing the rocks, you snub the saxifrage.
Three times, your flesh veers off like melted snow,
and thrice, your spirit forces it to trudge
back up. At last: the limestone crest. You turn,
not to the Pyrenees but to a page
of Augustine's *Confessions*. Put it down!
You seek your soul the way I sought the moon.
Feel the mistral sigh through firs and beeches;
watch the sun droop beneath the Rhône;
sip Syrah and pour some out for me:
I never let a poet drink alone.

Cela Xie

SAṂSĀRA

I saw bonsai in my father's garden,
their wood rippling within the wire,
writhing like dragons in their china,
turning blue, their surface cracked.
I saw the master, who ran his hand
along each branch and bent it back
so the skin was white with pressure,
and the spine almost showed teeth.
I was the one who kneeled in earth,
bearing the weight of my failed fruit
with the leaning column of my back.
I was carving after the gardener
when I forced my soul into this form,
both the prisoner and the torturer.

Jonathan Ukah

THE SINS OF MY FATHER

I grew into my father's name without doubt,
or guessed it too late to make a change.
But whose name should I bear hereafter?
It's the question that burns me to ashes;
since I am often mistaken for my father,
as though he has grown backwards,
like The Man Who Was Born Old.
There was a man with the head of a spear
who stopped me in the middle of a street.
He thought he had lost me forever
after I changed address without paying rent.
It took two police officers to clear the air
that I was not the reincarnation of my father.
A week later, I heard the crow of the raven,
then a splash of dust on my clothes,
my head swamped with bird's dung.
A woman informed me that my father,
who kept a catapult on our kitchen roof,
slaughtered ravens in the woods.
A dog saw me last month and began to bark,
wagging its tail and jumping on my trousers.
I froze in the heat and stared at the dog,
my face blank as glass, white as a wall,
before its owner exclaimed,
"Jimmy, coma here! It's not him!"
Jimmy thought that I was my father,
who lashed him with a club on a play day.
I stooped to caress Jimmy's neck
and assured him I was different
from the man whose face I inherited.
The day I dressed up for my wedding,
the sky was smiling at me with a million teeth,
and the sun bared its seven fingers on my head.

But there was thunder as I stepped out,
and I was drowning in the storm that came.
It was my mother who invented the idea I should hide
each time I walked under the moon.
My father killed the moon and injured the stars,
that's why they buried him in the water.

Zachary Daniel

FISHING COUSINS

The skin of the water shone like quartz
and when the sun sat low under the hills,
like jasper. When the tide dipped out pockets
of tadpoles could be found circling rock
hollows like captives. We fished bluegill,
walleye, knew the best spots to crook our poles,
how to wedge them in cracks of limestone
and let them sit 'til a line dipped long.

You taught me to flick the rod up
to set the hook and how to sit patient
as a prospector panning gold, how to
nonchalantly pluck a sprig of wild wheat
and hold it in the mouth, humming old
tunes your daddy taught you before
he chased some blonde to Dallas.

I think you hated that old shotgun house
and that's why we spent no time in it,
were too ashamed of your mom's Southern Baptist
supplications to look her in the face, hated the way
washed things never quite came out clean.

We found plates of shale or slate
and ate last night's bologna sandwiches
wrapped in wax paper, waded in creek
water up to our hips, lifted cigarettes
from your brother's dresser and under lips
tucked dip from his unlocked Ranger's
broken glove box. Our self-enforced curfew

was sundown, when light enough remained
to slip back through boxelder and sugar maple,
army crawl under rust red barbed wire

and shuffle thin through gaps in briar
only we had mapped, that would be lopped
back each summer; each summer the trail
we walked, it seemed, denser than ever.

Devon Brock

GYPSUM

When daybreak spades its slurry on the wall,
a perfection in gypsum quickens in my eye
and I ask myself if god labors in the trades,
and if there is delight in what would seem
a good day's work: an arabesque, a dance
swayed by what hardens far too soon.

Practiced in the art of the trowel, I imagine
a god fixed on its work, the wide arcs
of it, the crusted wrists, the muscled
strokes like rivers cut through on a plain
and gentle slope, knowing the end must be
a sheen with neither pit nor crease.

And when daybreak spades its slurry on the wall
I know I have been prepared for this—a life
upon which death would smear its tints
like a child or a Jackson Pollock. And if not that,
then the preferred hues of the day—the neutrals,
mute and hung with what might seem bucolic.

While I must admit that the stone, the gypsum
is ground elsewhere, I must also admit
that it is I who will smooth what I've come to
regard as a wall, and it is I who must press
the keys squarely into the laths nailed such
that they may at long last bear me up.

Zachary Daniel

SOMEWHERE IN WEST VIRGINNY

Snow on the hills, holly,
and a smattering
of beeches: the whole assemblage
resembles Pollock's
Blue Poles. An art critic
claimed that title
was "too distracting."
It's uncertain if a wooden horse
before the walls of Troy
is a curse or blessing,
if a javelin given
time to spear its target
lands harder than
a cannon's iron, if a spinal column
can apply to poems,
whether an Appalachian vista
matters or anything
beautiful at all.

J. M. Summers

BLACKBIRD

It would be unfair to call
it ugly: plain, perhaps,
would be a better word.
Commonplace, though the
colour of its feathers
is uncompromising in a
way the crow's is not.
Sitting atop the roof-
top it sings: calling
for a mate, marking
its territory. Wary only
of the judgements we
would make; its own veiled
behind the language it
speaks and we do not.
Alike, and not, defined
too by the difference
we note between ourselves.

Philip Dunkerley

TANAGER

I just had this recollection of the time I stood on your veranda
looking out between the plants that your green fingers had put there;
plants that always seemed to thrive. And then, in the small fruit tree
out on the street, beyond the gate, I saw a sayaca tanager,
a flash of gorgeous turquoise, teal and sapphire. And I thought
"What's such a dandy doing in a suburban street?" Then
it was gone; but the moment stayed, etched in my mind.
I associate it with you. Now you are gone too.

James Croal Jackson

UNDER THE SINK

In your dream you murdered me.
I am just happy you dreamt of me.
Carried chopped pieces
of me in your tote bag, hid me
under your sink among the grocery
bags and water stains. In the second
half of your dream, you said
I got out from under the sink
and said *I got you!* And I always
will, pieces of you I carry
with me, your proverbial
heart in mine, your eyes
locked in mine, your
subconscious wrestling
our not-so-tiny distance,
where when I moved
I thought you'd never think
of me, that what you'd carry
was the end, the sloppy end
with the broken bones,
the cut-up conversations,
the disjointed hugs in
summer heat, the space
we loved to share, daylight
hours a cool shade
of blue, a shield
in which we wished
for our shadows
to never escape
or at least hold
the other's fading
light. I never want
to be surprised

when our paths
cross next in life,
how I miss the days
you'd inhabit all my
dreams, days,
the whole field
and the entirety
beyond.

Alexander Etheridge

DECAY, DUST AND MOTHS

After Rolf Jacobsen

Under the bright hum of the city
a green decay spreads.
You can see its mossy reach
behind the tired faces of those you pass.
You can feel its black limbo
between busy words on the streets,
and in the staggers
of drifters and lost mothers.

Then everything slowly collapses
as dust—it hides in
the elements, in our DNA.
It creeps in our eyes
and in our minds, waiting for its day.
It is the oldest
kingdom—deep shadows
hide its patiently advancing troops.

Darkmoths wait at the city gates.
Deathmoths come up through
sewer grates. Nightmoths
flutter in our bad dreams.
From the empty temples
of heaven,
they fly in through our memories
into our rooms at night.
We hear the faded sound of freeways.
We learn the great spaces
of dust and decay. Gravemoths
lead us down to our silent home.

J. A. Marcus

COUNSEL FOR A CAVALIER

It is just a dream; not so much
changed. One night you were fevered, legs
cold as if ferried on a block of ice.

No hawk visited you but a midge,
and a moth so weak
it could have been a flake of ash.

You stood atop a tenement blinded
by the sun and saw only black
woods, nothing in detail, though

if you could—you say if you could
walk into that forest you'd find
your cold, bright lady warmed

by the embrace of a boar.
Find another woman, then;
find yourself a new jacket

and a new job and forget about it,
if you think you are the only one
with outsized desires. Forget about

the university, your whims
of travel—dull is the key when
the door is obsolete. When the road

at last rends your transmission into junk,
and you push by baby strollers,
dancing beggars and the obese to pass

a popular bistro, appraising
the myriad youthful faces
as delicate as porcelain,

you'll be just another cuckold
dreamer, too harried to know yourself,
even by the scent of flesh and herbs.

Devon Brock

THE KEPT THINGS

I keep willow switches,
knotted bits of string and fear,
sharper corners of gum wrapper chain,
and the long stuff of regret,
coiled
in a cardboard box,
in the haunch of my closet,
underneath my shirts,
underneath my shoes.

They are loud when I need them,
quiet, when not.

On some nights they shriek
and pound and twist.
But they have no teeth,
no hands. What worries me is
if I should burn them, or
bury them, would I not soon be found
sifting through ash, or
spading out a grave
with a spoon.

Zachary Daniel

EXHUMING THE DUCT TAPE MESSIAH, 1989

For Blaze Foley and Townes Van Zandt

I wanted you to have it, the guitar that had sat
in every pawnshop from here to Houston.
But folded like a penknife in my jacket pocket
is the ticket to reclaim it, and I am wedged
like a pebble, six feet under Texas clay,
in a coffin sealed with six strips of duct tape,
one for each friend that legged it
from the little white church in Austin
to the funeral south of Congress,
past the last tendrils of Onion Creek.
So when I heard the rumbling of the backhoe
ripping up the dirt, the headstone extruded
like a rotten molar, I knew you'd come
to let my baby sing again. You're the only one
who doesn't curse when the casket's opened.
What? He smells better now than living.
The flashlight in your left hand turns
my corpse as white as a holy relic.
And before you leave that pit with what you came for
clenched in your right, I hear you whisper
And I won't forget to put roses on your grave.

Shama

CAPTAIN MOONIKIN CAMPOS

NASA named him Moonikin,
and whizzed him into the night
to chase the Moon with eyes
which never opened.

With a plugged heart he bore
the twin disdain of his half-bodied crewmates
Helga and Zohar, and ignored the wires
winding his insides, for he was the commander
of the first manikin mission
which flew in November, twenty-twenty-two.

The din of love songs and lunar myths
lulled with the diminishing push and pull
of language as he hurtled out of gravity.
The Moon, which for millennia
has suffered human imagination,

approved his smart suit of blaze
and this new race of men: stoic,
mute, and plastic. Moonikin, stupefied
by this mad power, followed it to see

the aeons spread across the sky.
Meanwhile, here, morning swallowed
the Moon, and the birds opened their eyes:
chirrup, chirp, chirp.

D. A. Nicholls

BIRDSONG AT TEN THOUSAND FEET

Risen up into a minor satellite—
far above the city's glow, in blinking wingtip lights
that shuffle us in among stars
and bear us along the midnight flight's
arcing path—
you hear, as we all hear, the chitter
of sparrows that must line our metal wing
and the painted fuselage, fanning feathers idly
and turning tiny heads to sing
of early-Spring distraction—unhurried, serene,
a smaller breed of celestial—un-unsettled and unruffled
when we thought we'd gained such speed.

But hear their chirping and the scritch
of their small hops; see the land below,
littered with light, float by like dandelion seeds
in the lower, slower breeze that moves with the
little sparrow plumes, and blows to match their ease.

The chorus that sudden swells!
The notes that hold your veins! close like demure wings
across shy, chuckling beaks
—as in their eyes the stars wink
out and we are left with moon beams that streak
our sleek but bare and barren wings, and no sound at all
but groaning engines and the rush of foolish speed.

Devon Brock

THE PSEUDOLIPARIS

in the Izu–Ogasawara Trench

The deepest known snailfish

—half eel
—half tadpole

skin as clear as cellophane

—handless
—eyeless yet

bears the mold of water
on its spine—water
all ten billion pounds of it.

My mother was like that

—translucent
—her blue heart

crushed between her lungs

—pearled
—needled

—buoyant yet.

C.W. Bryan

ATOMS

Between atoms there is empty space—

My uncle pitches perfect horseshoes,
many widows gather to watch him throw.

Sunlight rests on the newly polished marble
of headstones—

Three stiff stalks of white roses lean
slightly eastward.

Washing your hands in hot water—

Bales of hay wrapped in tight blue cellophane
begin to hibernate until spring.

An electric current runs through the walls
of my home office—

What is in between empty space?

There is an immediacy to a handwritten letter
that cannot be explained by words alone—

My uncle did not always pitch perfect horseshoes.

Jonathan Ukah

IN THE BLADE OF TIME

This is my time, my chance, my hope,
my timelessness and timeliness in one,
when I want to be here and there
where the sea begins and the land ends,
or birds' songs start fresh green lawn;
I'm the sun that lifts a rose flower,
or the rain that drowns a high harvest;
the wind that scatters and sows seeds,
the delightful hand that shares food.
My present, past and future are dreams,
the conflux of life and death in a womb;
my beginning, end, another beginning
the face of a future without maps,
the start of joy and sorrow in a sling.
I'm stuck in the middle of one life,
still as a sea; floating as a river,
I await my time at the shrinking of a tide
when the clock of the apocalypse ticks
for death to holla from the top of a tree.
I dangle between hope and despair,
between destruction and construction;
I make, remake and unmake life,
create, desecrate and uncreate death,
yet I cannot build the wings to fly;
but in my head, all things are possible
and impossible in equal degrees.
When leaves fall, I whisper to the wind;
when storms fall on the branches of trees,
I lend them breath so they can dream,
and their dreams, when they are green,
are boundless like the breadth of the sea.
And now that we live in the deeds we yield,
there's time to make these seeds a gift.

John Grey

HENNY'S STORY

Henny would have fit right in unnoticed
except for the patent leather shoes
and that smell of French cologne
and the BMW of course,
the one that caused such a ruckus
when he parked it on an inner city street.

What was the point of making it big, he figured,
if you blended.
You couldn't just depend on the whispers
of people that you know.
Without the bling for example,
you were just one of the gang.

Henny's mother grew old and tired
worrying about him.
A roll of bills tossed on the table
and a directive to
"go buy yourself something"
didn't ease the pain any.
She knew any denomination over twenty
was blood money.

Nobody talks much about Henny now.
All the nickel bags,
the numbers he ran,
the loan-sharking,
the intimidation,
and his reputation barely registered
beyond that last arrest.

Men in suits came for him.
A crowd gathered
but his mother didn't leave her doorstep.

She watched that black car swallow him up
and it may as well have been a coffin.

Henny had an older brother
but he died in infancy.
In Danny's case,
the worst that could happen
only occurred the once.

C. W. Bryan

WHILE HIKING KENNESAW MOUNTAIN

The mountain fox takes the lead,
his wiry frame monolith-thin,
breaking the brush muzzle first
with the same sharp momentum
as a bayonet. He pares back April
to pad across the pinestraw,
prayer-quiet and practiced, like
so many Hail Marys before sunset.

Paul Jaskunas

A STREET CROSSING

In the beginning was the Word.
—John 1:1

A creed unspools across the sky.
A pentecostal wind, a blast of cloudcrest
lash an old woman on the curb,
her faith a gust of ancient air renewed.

Seized by the act of recalling
tomorrow, she halts in the crosswalk's
white bars. The heavy stoplight sways
and blinks, children scamper by.

She knows now what she will know
then, on the other side—knowledge
as frail as a newborn's breath, in and out,
dispersed, a ghost almost not seen,

yet felt, a chill in her chest.
The pavement of the street eddies
beneath her feet as a river's current does,
as Styx was said to caress the ferry.

A car horn honks, the day's design
wheels along. She scurries across
as the hour swings round again,
the usual imposition of minutes,

of errands and hungers, the shedding
of thought. She leaves behind, for now,
the summons of some transparent word,
the word for now a secret room

catacombed beneath time's palace,
or within an angel's light-filled womb,

a place forbidden, yearned for,
the untasted flavor of grace

encased as honey inside its comb,
the word, for now, an undiscovered home.

Jonathan Ukah

I AM A HEPHZIBAH

So thanksgiving is the foundation of worship,
a joyful noise, the celebration of glory;
but here is the valley of dry bones,
skull against skull, sinews against sinews,
and I cannot raise my voice beyond this sphere,
where darkness has slowly moved in,
stifled me to silence, struck me tame.
My praise cannot go to the grave
of flowers, waste and destruction,
the tomb of death, where there is nothing more
left to worship in the elevation of favour.
I dwell in the depths of sorrow and pain,
where thorns scratch my soft flesh,
and prickles abound in the vast void,
nothing green, so nothing grows,
except the march towards dust.
I feel the wide trenches in my heart,
yearning for fulfilment and delight.

Yet, I am thankful to have this hope
like a mustard seed seeping into my mouth;
each time, I want to curse my state
that gives no glory to my body,
those who, through flesh, invite fear.
So, I will arise like the rod of Aaron,
the dead and wooden staff of a man,
which blossoms after glory falls
like a tongue of flame from the sky,
and makes him the caretaker of his people.
The rod is fertile ground, flowers rising
flowers bringing forth fruit,
flowers producing seeds for eternity.
From this pit, I ascend towards Heaven

to become the delight of the Lord,
a Hephzibah, springing from desolation
to the throne of restoration
as my life of pain disappears like dew.

Jim Stewart

OCTOBER MORNING AFTER RAIN

You learn to see the light this way, before
dawn shatters the mirror puddles, the air
wrung out enough to blow dry the skunk
stripe you'd get crossing the bridge.
But the street glistens tintype silver
with headlights. The new garbage trucks
blink like Christmas lights, green, yellow,
red and green. The East River splashes
crazy, trying to jump the sea wall.
The RGB signs on the food truck
curve and spin sandwiches and drinks.
The city pouts in the mist
like Vaseline on the lens, looking
so much younger, more innocent, so like
a sucker, you give it another chance.

Leigh Doughty

APATHY REPORT

It was morning and light streamed through
the window as I sipped on my coffee.
The weather reporter's mouth smiled
without mirth as he told us:
"Floods in Bangladesh,
an earthquake in Taiwan,
severe blizzards across Estonia.
But here in London, it is
a bright and breezy day,
with glimpses of sunshine."
The world charmingly summarized
in a cheerful thirty-second burst.
Some are dying, and some drowning,
and some are freezing,
but everything was fine here
with the bad coffee and the sunlight
that was trying to get in.

PASTICCERIA ITALIANA

I walked into the pasticceria
and told the waitress that she had
made rather a poor show
and caused me no lack of
embarrassment.

She asked what I meant by this and I
told her that I had recommended this location to my wife,
but the doughnut they had sold her
had been undercooked on the inside.

She replied that it had probably been,
"short, rotund and ill-formed."

Only in Italian, the subject pronoun is omitted,
so I presumed she was describing my wife.

I responded that I was not aware that she had met my wife.

She said, "No, no, no, I meant the doughnut."

Diane Grey

WOULD YOU SOME TEA, MAYBE? IN THE KETTLE.

It's one of the great things about living
in such a low-rent place—the low rent itself aside—
the walls are thin and I get to
enjoy domesticities offered to my better-placed neighbors.
Maybe not better-placed; I've chosen to live here alone, and
I don't regret it. It's nice to walk
into a house with all the lights off and nothing
stirring and to be concerned for
a second, every day, before checking on
the bony cat sprawled near my bed.
Clean up the smells that shouldn't be there,
get my tie off and slump into this
television-facing sofa, a cup of
instant coffee in hand. Sipping in this silence
is something I wouldn't trade for all the doting I hear
these impressions of. I would be lying, though,
if I didn't say I hoped, every day, to come
home to another pair of eyes dancing,
a sloping song foreign to me playing,
a lie, offered in a voice that isn't just an echo.
One evening, maybe;
till then, alone.

D. H. Foster

ELYENA SAYS HI

Her Hi is always loud, an H with two vowels, *HA-EE*!
The die-cast Lightning McQueen she is puppeting says Hi.
The eyebrows of Gordon the train say Hi.
The zippered edge of her jacket waved in and out says Hi.

The Camaro outside her front passenger window says Hi.
The miles we have come and the hair band for the day say Hi.
The long hair floating in the bathtub says Hi.
Her latest age, eighteen, says Hi.

Between her fingers, my earlobe says Hi, and even
the air in some eye-height volume of the room says Hi.
The white pill does not say Hi, because we have ground it up in the pasta.
The *Magic Tree House* books she can read say Hi.

The fricatives she is missing don't say Hi.
James the train says *Mo*! when I ask if she wants to go outside.
The pinnate leaf of the mesquite on our walk (after all),
and the bees I point out round the bush say Hi.

Mom is *Maw*, but I am *Dæh*.
Yes is *Yeah*, No is *Mo*.
"O' the Indignity Gordon," her favorite one,
is counted out as *OH EE EE EE EE EE DOOR DOM*!

Elyena speaks with her AAC app sometimes:
I want Amy to come,
I want to swimming with Dad,
or, strangely, *Lightning McQueen is gas*.

Elyena's elaborate 5 by 7 by 18 inch Lego tower,
with all manner of arches and windows and spaces,
its engagements never coached, never modeled,
does not say Hi, she is intent.

When she is happy, she goes into her world and invites you.
Here the good will greet you with a cheerful Hello.
The bad are redeemed in the instant and do the same.
The non-existent are called forth to celebration.

But on days that bring protests and tears, she
is sorry, and we are sorry, and, Elyena, we are sorry
that we will die and that you will die.
But are we sorry that possibly the day will not come
in which your dreams are not made of trains?
We peer at the world, and it's all shuffling poems
out there, all adults dragging, wrangling
their deep, trainless burrows.

Shamik Banerjee

THE CONSTRUCTION LABOURERS

Before the newborn sun climbs to the crest
Of this numbed earth and night receives relief,
Their morning prayers and rituals are complete.
Their dress code's just a miry inner vest,
Pied loincloths, plus, at times, a handkerchief
Worn on the head to push the stinging heat
When they work on our terrace during noon.
Three rangy chaps, in this long month of June,

Are hired to renovate our second floor.
Sweat glistens on their skin as if fresh varnish
Spread on a wooden deck reflects its shine.
For lunch, they have white rice with water poured
On it, some fries; they like it plain, ungarnished.
And then, a flask of lemon tea is fine
To keep the flow of zing alive in them
Until it's time to leave at 5 p.m.

One in this group appears to be too young;
I wonder if he ever thinks of school.
The rest are middle-aged, so it seems.
While chewing betel, in an eastern tongue,
They talk about their village, little pool,
And farms. Their eyes display enormous dreams.
Three rawboned men far from their native place,
A hue of hope and longing on each face.

Jonathan Ukah

IF I BE A MAN

I could create victory out of every defeat,
or honour at the back of dishonour, recessed,
you who are invisible, in whom everything is visible;
one part of my back to celebrate your success,
the other, the shadow, is to mourn your failures;
something to die for and another thing to live for,
when life is a split image, a valley, or a phantom
with the depth of a mountain dancing on water,
and the shallowness of a river revving in the sky,
a desert like a dessert, dryness is wetness,
where the body wilts for the soul to flourish,
where the vanity of the substance is unsorted,
wriggles forward like the substance of the shadow;
and the surface assuming the light, the mirror
of the glitter through the underside.
Whatever lies beneath the ground is the place
where there is movement, where the hills rise;
it is what illuminates my life to the core,
though we live a life of dust and ashes
and of light shining through the pits of darkness.
There is no saving except through death,
no brokenness without being complete,
and the man who errs is the same who forgives.
If I am a man who runs and walks at the same time,
sleeps and wakes up in the thicket of the night,
if I kill an animal without a name, should I eat it or save it?
Let me not to the marriage of complexities,
where regret, doubt, sadness and hazard of my body
will find the air to blossom and multiply into despair.
Here, all impossibilities merge into possibilities,
and I'm rising like a phoenix when I'm falling.
Since my mother said that the power of life and death
was implanted on the tongue like teeth and gum,

I have decided to pluck out my tongue to spite my mouth;
there will be no dying through my tongue while I live.
If I were a man of few words, I would dive into the sea,
and emerge without a trace of water as a ghost.

Devon Brock

NOCTURNE

It is dark now and my living room is the stern cabin
of an ancient ship. Two candles swing in the hurricanes
under the bulkheads, as through the gallery the wake divides,
both right and sinister. History upon history rolls
behind under moonlight. The north wind bulges
gale-force about the house. The window panes shake,
and the town around me is a fleet of foundering boats,
battered, adrift upon a hillside, migrant rafts among them
made absurd by hay rolls bobbing as mines
in a bay risen with snowmelt.

C.W. Bryan

REMINISCING OUT MY BEDROOM WINDOW

It's a night so dark,
I think the sun may just give it all up.

I believe it is going to rain.

The waking world arrived late today—
the rooster with the belting voice
was found broken-winged, dog-bitten, spackled with blood.

In her dreams beside me,
she begins to sweat, as if climbing
a ceaseless ladder out of herself.

Rung by rung she awakens.

A stillness swaddles the world
as a mewling baby—
the momentum-killer.

Some people are just born that way,
they can't help it, you said.

A thousand exhales—
the wind picks up against the leaves,
and rain begins to fall.

Devon Brock

CIRCULAR, LIKE A BREEZE

I will not give my heartbreak
to a river or a browning flower
or a cloud dissembling
in the stratosphere. It will remain
right here, not like a tumor,
not like a dim city risen
from the plains—steel on steel,
story on story: firm by a lake—
but in the shade of someone
barely seen, slipping in then out
of this, gracious if not cunning,
wounded and lithe, having no more
form than a tremor or a half-
remembered laugh, no more form
than an unheld hand or a warm breeze.

Seth Strickland

"MY FATHER DIDN'T SEE"

My father didn't see the possum trundling
to whatever possum night-business it would go to.
Its spine, its flesh, skeleton, especially the skull moved
the car, which was large, even by American standards.
The half-pleasant errand conversation there stopped.
I looked back, hoping to see anything but movement,
hoping the candle of life had been snuffed so utterly
that there wasn't smoke.

Zachary Daniel

HOW A POEM IS WRITTEN

Under some spell, perhaps, the wind
lifts its huge hand
and stirs a chime, which like the music
of some battered shell
dislodged from the sand
comes to our ears in the form of a bird
passing above a few clouds.

Zachary Daniel

BEACHCOMBING

This beach
is full of flaws.
The ribs and the jaws
of one million half
and empty shells
pock this stretch of surf,
but like a grain of sand
when angled
and examined,
their origin
can be determined:
cockleshell or calico,
abalone or nautilus.
One must know
when dealing with
an intertidal harvest
what counts for gold
and what isn't worth
its weight in hardness.
The chaff gets discarded;
all value's in the pick
and prod, the honesty
of process.

Donald Goodbrand Saunders

ARIADNE ON NAXOS

"Just a business trip," he said. "I'll be back
before you know I'm gone."
Ariadne no longer bothers
to look out to sea.

In the shade of a beach bar
her back is to the Aegean,
her horizons now bottles
of raki, retsina, ouzo.

She's a tolerated fixture.
Tourists from the mainland
love to hear her stories,
those twisted, amazing tales

of palace intrigue, scandal,
affairs and betrayals
and some weird monster stuff
(crazy, but she spins a great yarn)

and the words pour out as long
as her glass is topped up.
But from time to time
she falls silent.
        Two images
are contending for memory:

Ariadne on the shore
waving off her lover
till the black sails vanish.

Ariadne at a dark portal
reeling in a cord gone suddenly slack.
Seeing the frayed end,

she allows a thin smile.

The corners of her labyrinth
were so hard
and so sharp.

Adam Haver

COASTAL MORNING

I slept in the old car last night, the one
rusted by the onshore breeze, stranded
with a broken windscreen and no keys.

A storm swept in, soaked my sight as I
slept, so I have decided, on a whim, that
it is better if I bathe in the still-raging sea

and climb the cliff in the bay that
oversees the kittiwakes, who make their
nests in crevices of white-stained stone.

I have attempted vagary for so many years,
but now that I state this aloud, I feel a
sudden wildness—it is time to risk it all.

Paul Jaskunas

THE OPEN WINDOW

After the painting by Pierre Bonnard

May no hand shut Bonnard's window.
May the air always gush into his room,
that sacristy of color where his lover
in the shadowed corner dreams
a black cat into being.

Painted hand to painted paw,
they greet each other, co-conspirators
in conjuring the sumptuous sky and oaks
beyond the sill. Bonnard,

however fervent the wish, do not
put down your brush
to kiss her on her smiling mouth.
Her spell mustn't be broken.
The perfection of the world
depends upon her peace.

Leave your lover be in the pastel room
awash in the abiding light of desire.

Zachary Daniel

ADVICE TO A YOUNG POET

Let your rugs be tapestries
where your feet tack them to the floor.

Let flowers sprout from the crater
in your bed, daffodils and mums.

Let your silence be a drum,
little man. The pulse of centuries

burns beneath your skin like a swatch
of steel wool touched by a match.

Let the girl burn the lake
with the reflection of her red slicker

or a lover turn the page of your manuscript
with her breath. Let the little brass knob

pull out a drawer
to another world.

D. H. Foster

PUBLIC BURDEN: REPLACING THE BULB

Eight hundred fifty lumens,
twenty seven hundred Kelvin—
these precious clues I have deciphered
from ink-blurred 4-point type
on the cold body,
on its tapered neck.

At lonely high noon my great plastic cart
rolls slowly
into the aisle contested by cartels of bulbs:
LEDs in sundry diffusive globes,
cloaked in five-color boxes with nine fonts.
Silver triangle corners, pictures of dining rooms,
words such as "Natural," "Enhanced," "Comfort," "Precision."

But "800 Lumens"
is like "Men's Shampoo" and "Fluoride Toothpaste."
Every forthright word is embarrassed, crouched up to the decor,
like it was the news in the News, like it was a tell-tale earring
awaiting day sergeant Sidney and his metal detector.

Shamik Banerjee

SCENES IN MAY

Prostrated stray dogs of these lanes
Look half-deceased; dust on the ground
    Envelops them from gut to chest.
    And when the noon sun does its best,
They find respite in open drains,
As water's nowhere to be found.

Just past a field that's not too far
And once a home to crocuses,
    A chockablock, old market street
    (With fly-stormed briskets parched by heat)
Stinks up the air. The buyers are
Like vultures flocked near carcasses.

By rail tracks, homeless people sleep
Beside hard beds of hot granite.
    Unclad and scorched from feet to hands
    Like corpses on cremation lands,
They dwell with no relief to keep
Each white-hot day and foodless night.

DW Baker

VASCULAR

blue like currents
red like blood
lattice network

one by one
blue like death screen
red like flash

4D lenses
looking glass
blue like glowing

red like hot
needle sewing
neon spots

blue like oceans
red like Mars
interstellar

carbon scars
blue like piercing
red like pain

grieving heartland
maxed out brain
blue like twelve bars

red like beat
tachycardic
Venus heat

DW Baker

VERDIGRIS

gold like backlit
green like moss
molten statue

pour the dross
gold like five star
green like home

single sunlamp
heat-lapse bomb
gold like ancient

green like wild
strong force latent
inner child

gold like ages
green like spring
revolution

finds the king
gold like privilege
green like god

ever present
body song
gold like chosen

green like found
carbon life forms
in the ground

Marka Rifat

THE BATTLE IS LONG LOST

It would rise between the toes of dinosaurs:
horsetail, pernicious rhizome creeping,
speeding, spreading, inexorable, nine feet below.
A tiny fragment will launch a new invasion.

Horsetail, pernicious rhizome creeping—
only rock and Roundup divert its path.
A tiny fragment will launch a new invasion.
Fear the supreme leader of nature's thugs.

Only rock and Roundup divert its path:
dead men's fingers too mild a term.
Fear the supreme leader of nature's thugs.
You will go mad fighting equisetum.

Dead men's fingers too mild a term.
It would rise between the toes of dinosaurs.
You will go mad fighting equisetum—
speeding, spreading, inexorable, nine feet below.

Grace Atlas

TWO TOURISTS AS ROMULUS AND REMUS

Tepid and infantless, a stork perches
atop the ruins of the temple of Artemis.
The steppes behind us nurture a lone
poppy, fire-red. Fresco fragments
litter the halls; some are gods,
others battleplans.
We are enraptured. Like an oracle,
a scene beckons: two men stoic
atop a ruined city. The temple
fractures. The stork flees.
Fire drips from the divine bust,
We would burn Rome for her.
I would burn Rome again.

David Elliot Eisenstat

AUTUMN IN TORONTO

A wasp hangs from my balcony rail, wriggling
against a ruined web. I spot the fly
she meant to feed her sisters—they feed her
their sweet secretions. Soon, they will decamp
from spit-and-wood-pulp hexes she helped build.
Below, the highway is a cocktail straw
where lines of weary cars are bubbling home.
TVs flick on in glass towers. She stops.
Should I have done something? At Sunday brunch,
I shooed a wasp from my hot toddy; her,
perhaps; but that was of no consequence—
workers always perish in the frost.
And anyway, the asters will provide.
When I look back from my TV, she's gone.

Terry Trowbridge

APRIL EXTREMES

We Canadians forget
plums trees blossom
in the cold April rainstorms
and birds build their nests
by weaving between extremes.

Building shelter is building resistance.
Birds who fly in daring murmuration
value stillness by sewing cupolas.
Nest is the opposite of sky.
Blossom petals grow, as do snowflakes;
even the last snow of the final flurry.

C. W. Bryan

CULLING SEASON

My short apple tree moves in the garden, coming
or going draped in a white smock. Its blossoms swan-
like swim in the current of air. I have brought the axe.
No fruit or friction throws their
pithy judgment my way. I myself am the reaper
of my grandfather's sowing. He once prayed at church
every Sunday, twice on Easter.

I have his hooked nose that presses on the glass
of every window where the sun rises, the transparency
only visible by the stolen oil of my face. It glistens
as if anointed. I myself am culled,
cursed not by generations yet, but by the breeze
as it slowly persists like a shaded snowbank.
Two years the moonstruck eye of an oil lantern
roared in the window, its flame heckled by
a stiff breeze that moved with all the urgency
of Iphigenia, all the innocence.

Under the lily-shadow of the moon-blackened lake,
the silver-breasted cob floats, the cold wind sliding
off his smooth lapels, his thick chest a dam
for his copper children as they thrash wildly behind,
seeking the lighthouse safety of a windbreak. It comes
in the form of a hundred-year promise. The apples
hang loosely far above them.

From my porch, we breathe the same air. A sound
like a whetstone at my approach. The fowl
huddle into themselves, nestled like clover
at the base of the tree. I have never
swung this axe, seen its iron half-moon
pare the wind as easily as an orange. It glistens
with expectations, rings with jubilation as it tears

the gray bark away with its incisors. The first
apple falls, but the birds will not scare.

Max Roland Ekstrom

INNOVATION AND IMPACT: TWO TWENTIETH-CENTURY JOURNALS

Influence and longevity are not synonymous for literary journals. It's hard to think of a journal with more meteoric impact than *The Egoist*, named in honor of Fredrich Nietzsche's philosophy of the individual. During its short five-year run between 1914 and 1919, founding editor Dora Marsden advanced a new vision for literature, publishing James Joyce, T.S. Eliot, William Carlos Williams, Robert Frost, H.D., Marianne Moore, Charlotte Mew, and Ezra Pound. The poets and writers published were not professors; some lived hand-to-mouth. The editor's own qualification was a college degree and a stint in jail for peaceful protesting. She was a feminist, and for her, the next step in advancing women's liberty was in the realm of language.

We credit William Carlos Williams for the Modernist credo "no idea but in things," his call for poetry to ground itself in image and discard flowery language. But it was Dora Marsden, not Williams, who first declared war on hollow verbiage. In a 1915 essay, "I Am" (*The Egoist* vol. 2, no. 1), Marsden declares: "Our war is with words and in their every aspect: grammar, accidence, syntax: body, blood, and bone." She argues language presently functions to oppress, not express: "words have developed into a 'Culture' and grown masters of all and servants of none."

The magazine debuted with the subtitles "An individualist Review" and "Formerly the New Freewoman," on the first day of the year 1914. The premier issue opened with Marsden's invective against the English state as hypocritical and repressive, consisting of conceptual "veils," such as Liberty and Democracy, that are "feeble and faded." In retrospect, on the eve of World War I, with democracies prepared to ship innumerable young men to the slaughter, her essay feels prophetic.

The poetry of the debut issue likewise foretells things to come, despite F.S. Flint's forgettable effort. Flint's free verse feels weak beside the existing superstructure of formal meter:

London, my beautiful
is not the sunset
nor the pale green sky
simmering through the curtain
[...]

Compare it to Landor's appeal to sentiment a generation earlier (e.g., "Late Leaves"):

The leaves are falling; so am I;
The few late flowers have moisture in the eye;
    So have I too.
Scarcely on any bough is heard
Joyous, or even unjoyous, bird
    The whole wood through.

The Victorian could employ iambic variation as a chiaroscuro to complicate what would otherwise register as cliché. Flint also approaches sentiments that are hardly particular to him and are intended to express a common feeling. But his free-verse, by comparison, lies flat on the page.

Modernism would eventually shatter the idea of an easy unity of feeling among what the Victorians would deem "civilized" people. But Marsden would need fiercer soldiers to further her attack on civilization's myths and deceptions. William Carlos Williams took his best shot in issue number six, put to press March 16th. "The Wanderer: A Rococo Study" is also a city portrait, but it disposes of Flint's expectation of unity by alluding to, and attempting to dismantle, Walt Whitman's "Crossing Brooklyn Ferry". The four-part poem asks the question under its "Advent" section (the "she" here is a vision of a "young crow" introduced in the preceding stanza):

But one day crossing the ferry
With the great towers of Manhattan before me,
Out at the prow with the sea-wind blowing
I had been wearying many questions
Which she had put on to try me:
How shall I be a mirror to this modernity?

Williams has injected himself into the Whitman role of interpreter and medium of his age, attempting to form a poetry that would speak for the broadest possible cross-section of America (and indeed, in this instance, beyond). But according to Marsden's high Nietzschean standard, it would not be enough to simply echo America's free-verse everyman. Williams would have to overcome him. That would have to wait, as Williams stumbles over his feminine endings and endline assonance, unable to sharpen his imagery into the gemlike clarity he accomplishes later in *Spring and All*.

Marsden's tenure at the helm of *The Egoist* was brief, and her last issue as head editor would be June 15th. (It's possible she required more time to care for her sick mother in Southport.) That issue continues the serialization of James Joyce's *A Portrait of an Artist as a Young Man*, started in February, and turns *The Times Literary Supplement* into a source of comedy by quoting its pretentiousness out of context as "Revelations:" "Poetry in Germany has a very ancient history;" "For too many people the cooking of breakfast in the early morning is peevish work;" and "The book is worthy of its publishers."

In later issues, Marsden would continue to pen editorials on women's suffrage but would no longer focus on the exhausting task of preparing manuscript for publication twice per month. Indeed, Harriet Shaw Weaver, her successor and a crucial patron of the magazine, reduced the frequency to monthly, granting herself and her staff more time to secure and copyedit material between issues. As the focus of the magazine continued to shift from politics to letters, quality over quantity proved exceedingly wise.

Ironically, Dora Marsden created a platform for some men whose work and lives didn't align with her values. To call Eliot and Pound "chauvinists" is certainly warranted—Eliot in his penchant for circulating offensive doggerel, and Pound for advancing fascism, with its cold scorn for female agency. But maybe that is too much of a 21th-century concern. We are the ones who feel a need to assign such labels to public personas. Marsden had no such compunction. Her goal was to liberate language, and by any measure, she succeeded.

§

Ploughshares, one of the most influential journals founded in the late 20th century, also carried a whiff of insurrection, thanks to its origins in Irish Boston. In 1971, DeWitt Henry, then an aspiring novelist, Harvard grad, and Iowa Writers Workshop alumnus, partnered with the publican of a Cambridge pub, Irish émigré Peter O'Malley. They named the magazine for the bar, the Plough and Stars, in tribute to the Seán O'Casey play of the same name. The play, dramatizing events of the 1916 Easter Rising, had inspired a riot at the Abbey Theatre in Dublin, in 1926.

The contemporary Troubles in Northern Ireland eerily presaged Boston's own difficulties with school integration in the wake of the Racial Imbalance Act of 1965, ratified by the Massuchesetts statehouse, that recognized Boston's de facto school segregation as unconstitutional. When the Boston School Committee stonewalled Black families and refused to integrate, civil rights leaders organized, protested, and took legal action. Court-ordered bussing ensued in the '70's, resisted by counterprotests, racial violence, and rioting.

Meanwhile, expatriate Irish nationalism found odd bedfellows with communists, artists, activists, and the radical intellectual vanguard. Once again, the undercurrents of anti-establishment politics combined explosively with shifting tides in aesthetics. High Modernism had become moribund. A new path forward was called for.

The debut issue was heavily Celtic in flavor, featuring Dublin poets Hugh Maxton, Hayden Murphy, and Thomas Redshaw. Boston talent was distinguished by Tom Lux, Sidney Goldfarb, William Corbett, and George Kimball. However, it is Anne Waldman's Catullan masterpiece, "Sophisticated Poem," that best captures the young-people energy of a brand-new enterprise: "2 words / fucking / & sucking."

Ploughshares seized the day, ingesting and metabolizing the shift in literary power happening all around it. Harvard University had produced a generation of America's major male poets (and they were only men; Harvard did not enroll women until 1977), such as W.S. Merwin, Richard Wilbur, Robert Lowell, Donald Hall, John Ashbery, and Frank O'Hara. But rival centers of power were emerging, including in New York and San Francisco. Increasingly, Harvard wasn't the sole gatekeeper, as Iowa Writers

Workshop supplanted it as the ticket to agents and book deals. The workshop model was toppling the traditional power dynamic of the lecture and seminar. At Iowa, the poets were teaching one another.

Poets of the Vietnam era, brimming with suspicion at institutional authority, looked to create a literary culture that subverted it. Henry and O'Malley's inspired act of rebellion was to enforce a policy of rotating editors—a nod to their communistic ideals. They recruited volunteer staff editors to read submissions and canvass their contacts for material, but prospective writers could not predict who would have the final say. This decision to collectivize editorial effort while eliminating any permanent editorial authority proved seminal.

Over the next three years, they infused the Harvard Yard milieu with new blood via James Tate, William Meredith, Charles Wright, Susan Howe, William Dickey, Andre Dubus II, Raymond Carver, Anthony Hecht, Robert Pinsky, Elizabeth Bishop, Maxine Kumin, James Merrill, Mark Strand, and Sam Cornish. But Harvard talent was featured, too, including a mix of stalwarts and new faces, such Robert Lowell, Richard Wilbur, Frank Bidart, Jonathan Aaron, Peter Davison, and Helen Vendler. From the beginning, *Ploughshares* cultivated a cosmopolitan intelligence, plucking superb translations of Mahmoud Darwish, Octavio Paz, Carlos Drummond de Andrade, and Eugenio Montale.

Unlike *The Egoist*, *Ploughshares*, with its swirl of guest editors and teeming anthill of industrious staff, had no stated ideology. Because so many of its early contributors indeed doubled as staff, the journal provided a natural way for young poets to make connections. Just as Dora Marsden's feminism provided a critical spark to Modernism, Peter O'Malley's Irish-Americanism touched off a chain reaction.

But what, exactly, was the movement *Ploughshares* contributed to? Certainly, surrealism, postmodernism, and post-confessionalism filtered through those early issues, with poems that point toward things to come from Tate, Lux, Pinsky, Wright, and Howe. American verse would increasingly specialize in minor revelation and personal crises, revisiting French Symbolism and Beat poetry with an eye to more refined and exacting surrealism. But that was merely the water that ran under its bridge.

Ploughshares published the best poetry it could get its hands on, according to whatever criteria made sense at the time. No guest editor could meaningfully shape the staff's practices, never mind hire or fire. Power devolved to the staff, who out of necessity took a utilitarian stance, absent any other. Its guiding star would not be Nietzsche's continental egoism but John Dewey's American pragmatism.

Ploughshares' ideals were vague enough that its submitters and editors could project whatever they wished for literature onto it—especially if what they wanted was their own importance. The journal was supposedly taste-agnostic, and thus theoretically a neutral arbiter. This appearance of impartiality made it a sought-after academic credential, and an ideal clearinghouse for American literary pedigree.

Henry and O'Malley were consistent, turning out issue after issue of the best writers in America for the better part of two decades. Rather than wage war against the existing system, they subsumed it. The *Ploughshares* star continued to rise as MFA programs popped up all over the country, looking to hire faculty with the right publications to their names. Henry himself took a post at Emerson College teaching Creative Writing in 1984 and threw himself into the work of building up the program. (I received my MFA from Emerson College in 2004.) Henry secured tenure in 1989 and assumed the departmental chair. According to his memoir, *Endings and Beginnings* (MadHat Press, 2021), Henry pitched the college on the merits of acquiring *Ploughshares*, and O'Malley sold his share of the *Plough* to the college for an undisclosed sum, leaving Henry lone captain.

Going into a departmental meeting to renew his chairmanship, Henry assumed the vote would be a formality. "I had accomplished miracles in hiring, in curriculum, and in enrollments, to everyone's benefit. If there were soreheads in my fold, I had them well outnumbered..." He had miscalculated. The engine of meritocracy that Henry had so assiduously oiled was too important for any one man to control, and perhaps his colleagues sensed that. "At this point, 5-4, my faculty voted against my renewal as department chair...I was also forced to surrender any real role in *Ploughshares* as my protege took full control."

Don Lee took the helm at Ploughshares and continued to run it in much the same manner, with guest-star editors promoting the title while throwing readers off any particular aesthetic scent. But the journal had already served its purpose. It had wrested away Harvard University's exclusive right to knight poets. Going forward, that would have to be done by committee, one safely institutionalized just across the river from the Plough and Stars.

§

Like Marsden, Henry, and O'Malley, young poets and writers today are also frustrated by the literary establishment's inability to connect with and respond to the political moment. They want journals to stake their reputations against local and global injustices, and they call for existing institutional structures to be swept aside, even if they're not exactly sure what to replace them with. In June of 2020, the board of the Poetry Foundation, *Poetry*'s institutional backer, resigned in the wake of the George Floyd killing. The final straw was a petition signed by thousands online that stated, in part, "we dream of a world in which the massive wealth hoarding that underlies the foundation's work would be replaced by the redistribution of every cent to those whose labor amassed those funds." Similar activism precipitated the implosion of the online journal *Guernica*, due to its decision to run a piece about the Gaza war from an Israeli perspective.

No literary journal today, however big or small, has much influence on public policy. The people who read it may be swayed by its contents, but are unlikely to rise to action. Its poems and stories, no matter how affecting, lie far downstream from the political energies that first inspired its founders. Today's journals can only offer words, and the professors in charge of them—as most of these journals are run by academics—must fill their calendars not with freedom fighting but with departmental meetings.

Zadie Smith, novelist and professor of Creative Writing at NYU, was recently asked by Ezra Klein about our era's fixation on language, terminology, and politically correct speech ("Zadie Smith on Populists, Frauds and Flip Phones," *New York Times*, 9/17/24). She replied:

> It was a linguistic turn mostly on the part of young people. But how can you blame them? Given that they had no money, really, no tools, very

little physical, material freedoms in the world, it seems natural to me that they fought in the only place they knew where to fight, which was language. The actual means of production are out of their hands.

Certainly, some young people *do* have money and *do* have tools—the freshman class's age at Harvard and NYU is still well under 30, and in aggregate suffers no lack of financial resources. It's not the young or the poor who are paying lip-service.

Revisit any issue of *The Egoist* and there can be no doubt what the journal's goals were. It fought a war, sometimes winning, sometimes losing, against conditionalized thought. The same cannot be said of *Ploughshares*. Its 18-year independent run was not a struggle over language, but who should own the means of producing it.

Today, with print-on-demand and Web publishing requiring little or no capital, it doesn't take a lot of money and tools to get started. And many do. But a small number of elite journals maintain an effective monopoly on producing the literary credentials required to build a career and make money in the field. That is a monopoly of the means of production that Marsden would surely recognize as no less hypocritical than any of the others maintained for the advantage of the few at the expense of the many.

Ploughshares' first issue contained a poem by Tom Lux entitled "The Cave or The Mine." In 1971, Lux's signature lineation—enjambing nearly everything and fracturing phrases at arbitrary parts of speech—could likely still raise an eyebrow. Now, in the hands of a thousand pale imitators, the technique is more often a triumph of style over substance, of eye over ear. But here, it plays toward the speluncaphobia of the piece:

> [...] No matter
> where you are you can drop to your
> knees and hear the damp invitations,
> the buzzing of a hollow, silent place.
> You'd rather think of it as a mine.
> Men go down in mines, they come up,
> they go down again. Caves are slightly
> different. Some caves have never been

visited. There is something uncertain
about caves. But you can't stop the
person underground who is always fol-
lowing you. You can't stop a buried
shadow. [...]

As the "you" of the poem becomes aware of a Dantean world below and its mysterious shadow figure, the poem toys with an ambiguity—is it a cave, like Plato's, perhaps, containing a fire? Or is it a mine, in which the industrious toil in search of value?

Lux never intended to do so, but I can't help but seize the dichotomy he presents as not merely an *ars poetica*, but also as two models for the collective act of literary production. The mine and the cave may at first seem similar as we go about our business above them. But if we stop to listen carefully, ear to the earth, they couldn't be more different. A cave conjures our most primitive origins, and in the philosophical context, it holds possibilities of both deception and enlightenment. By contrast, a mine is a place where resources, both human and natural, are exploited until they are all used up.

The Pierian is only possible with the financial support of poets, readers, and friends. If you wish to join them in supporting our mission, please visit www.patreon.com/thepierian for more information, or use the QR code below.

Milton Keynes UK
Ingram Content Group UK Ltd.
UKHW050817181124
2908UKWH00070B/797

9 798330 503667